MW01241821

**Wood-Block**

**by F. Morley Fletcher,**

In issuing these volumes of a series of Handbooks on the Artistic Crafts, it will be well to state what are our general aims.

In the first place, we wish to provide trustworthy text-books of workshop practice, from the points of view of experts who have critically examined the methods current in the shops, and putting aside vain survivals, are prepared to say what is good workmanship, and to set up a standard of quality in the crafts which are more especially associated with design. Secondly, in doing this, we hope to treat design itself as an essential part of good workmanship. During the last century most of the arts, save painting and sculpture of an academic kind, were little considered, and there was a tendency to look on "design" as a mere matter of appearance. Such "ornamentation" as there was was usually obtained by following in a mechanical way a drawing provided by an artist who often knew little of the technical processes involved in production. With the critical attention given to the crafts by Ruskin and Morris, it came to be seen that it was impossible to detach design from craft in this way, and that, in the widest sense, true design is an inseparable element of good quality, involving as it does the selection of good and suitable material, contrivance for special purpose, expert workmanship, proper finish, and so on, far more than mere ornament, and indeed, that ornamentation itself was rather an exuberance of fine workmanship than a matter of merely abstract lines. Workmanship when separated by too wide a gulf from fresh thought--that is, from design--inevitably decays, and, on the other hand, ornamentation, divorced from workmanship, is necessarily unreal, and quickly falls into affectation. Proper ornamentation may be defined as a language addressed to the eye; it is pleasant thought expressed in the speech of the tool.

In the third place, we would have this series put artistic craftsmanship before people as furnishing reasonable occupations for those who would gain a livelihood. Although within the bounds of academic art, the competition, of its kind, is so acute that only a very few per cent. can fairly hope to succeed as painters and sculptors; yet, as artistic craftsmen, there is every probability that nearly every one who would pass through a sufficient period of apprenticeship to workmanship and design would reach a measure of success.

In the blending of hand-work and thought in such arts as we propose to deal with, happy careers may be found as far removed from the dreary routine of hack labour as from the terrible uncertainty of academic art. It is desirable in every way that men of good education should be brought back into the productive crafts: there are more than enough of us "in the city," and it is probable that more consideration will be given in this century than in the last to Design and Workmanship.

* * * * *

There are two common ways of studying old and foreign arts--the way of the connoisseur and the way of the craftsman. The collector may value such arts for their strangeness and scarcity, while the artist finds in them stimulus in his own work and hints for new developments.

The following account of colour-printing from wood-blocks is based on a study of the methods which were lately only practised in Japan, but which at an earlier time were to some degree in use in Europe also. The main principles of the art, indeed, were well known in the West long before colour prints were produced in Japan, and there is some reason to suppose that the Japanese may have founded their methods in imitating the prints taken from Europe by missionaries. Major Strange says: "The European art of chiaroscuro engraving is in all essentials identical with that of Japanese colour-printing.... It seems, therefore, not vain to point out that the accidental sight of one of the Italian colour-prints may have suggested the process to the Japanese." The Italians aimed more at expressing "relief" and the Japanese at flat colour arrangements; the former used oily colours, and the latter fair distemper tints; these are the chief differences. Both in the West and the East the design was cut on the plank surface of the wood with a knife; not across the grain with a graver, as is done in most modern wood engraving, although large plank woodcuts were produced by Walter Crane and Herkomer, about thirty years ago, as posters.

The old woodcuts of the fifteenth century were produced as pictures as well as for the illustration of books; frequently they were of considerable size. Often, too, they were coloured by stencil plates or freely by hand.

At the same time the printing in colour of letters and other simple devices in books from wood-blocks was done, and a book printed at St. Albans in 1486 has many coats of arms printed in this way; some of the shields having two or three different colours.[1]

About the year 1500 a method of printing woodcuts in several flat tones was invented in Germany and practised by Lucas Cranach and others. A fine print of Adam and Eve by Hans Baldung in the Victoria and Albert Museum has, besides the bold black "drawing," an over-tint printed in warm brown out of which sharp high lights are cut; the print is thus in three tones.

[1] See R. M. Burch, Colour Printing, 1900.

Ugo da Carpo (c. 1480-1530) working in Venice, introduced this new type of tone woodcut into Italy; indeed, he claimed to be the inventor of the method. "This was called chiaroscuro, a name still given to it, and was, in fact, a simple form of our modern chromo printing." His woodcuts are in a simple, vigorous style; one of them after Raphael's "Death of Ananias," printed in brown, has a depth and brilliancy which may remind us of the mezzo-tints of Turner's Liber Studiorum. This is proudly signed, "Per Ugo da Carpo," and some copies are said to be dated 1518.

Andrea Andreani (c. 1560-1623), a better known but not a better artist, produced a great number of these tone woodcuts. Several prints after Mantegna's "Triumphs of Caesar" have a special charm from the beauty of the originals; they are printed in three tints of grey besides the "drawing"; the palest of these tints covers the surface, except for high lights cut out of it. A fine print of a Holy Family, about 15?8 inches, has a middle tone of fair blue and a shadow tint of full rich green. Copies of two immense woodcuts at the Victoria and Albert Museum, of Biblical subjects, seem to have been seems to cramp the hand and injure the eyes of all but the most gifted draughtsmen. It is desirable to cultivate the ability to seize and record the "map-form" of any object rapidly and correctly. Some practice in elementary colour-printing would certainly be of general usefulness, and simpler exercises may be contrived by cutting out with scissors and laying down shapes in black or coloured papers unaided by any pattern.

Finally, the hope may be expressed that the beautiful art of wood-cutting as developed in Western Europe and brought to such perfection only a generation ago is only temporarily in abeyance, and that it too may have another day.

W. R. LETHABY. September 1916.

AUTHOR'S NOTE

This little book gives an account of one of the primitive crafts, in the practice of which only the simplest tools and materials are used. Their method of use may serve as a means of expression for artist-craftsmen, or may be studied in preparation for, or as a guide towards, more elaborate work in printing, of which the main principles may be seen most clearly in their application in the primitive craft.

In these days the need for reference to primitive handicrafts has not ceased with the advent of the machine. The best achievements of hand-work will always be the standards for reference; and on their study must machine craft be based. The machine can only increase the power and scale of the crafts that have already been perfected by hand-work. Their principles, and the art of their design, do not alter under the machine. If the machine disregards these its work becomes base. And it is under the simple conditions of a handicraft that the principles of an art can be most clearly experienced.

The best of all the wonderful and excellent work that is produced to-day by machinery is that which bears evidence in itself of its derivation from arts under the pure conditions of classic craftsmanship, and shows the influence of their study.

The series of which this book is a part stands for the principles and the spirit of the classic examples. To be associated with those fellow-craftsmen who have been privileged to work for the Series is itself an honour of high estimation in the mind of the present writer. If the book contributes even a little toward the usefulness of the series the experiments which are recorded here will have been well worth while.

To my friend Mr. J. D. Batten is due all the credit of the initial work. He began the search for a pure style of colour-printing, and most generously supported and encouraged my own experiments in the Japanese method.

To my old colleague Mr. A. W. Seaby I would also express my indebtedness for his kind help and advice.

F. M. F.

EDINBURGH COLLEGE OF ART, September 1916.

CONTENTS

CHAPTER I

Introduction and Description of the Origins of Wood-block Printing--Its Uses for Personal Artistic Expression, for Reproduction of Decorative Designs, and as a Fundamental Training for Student of Printed Decoration

CHAPTER II

WOOD-BLOCK PRINTING

BY THE

JAPANESE METHOD

CHAPTER I

INTRODUCTORY

Introduction and Description of the Origins of Wood-block Printing; its uses for personal artistic expression, for reproduction of decorative designs, and as a fundamental training for students of printed decoration.

The few wood-block prints shown from time to time by the Society of Graver Printers in Colour, and the occasional appearance of a wood-block print in the Graver Section of the International Society's Exhibitions, or in those of the Society of Arts and Crafts, are the outcome of the experiments of a small group of English artists in making prints by the Japanese method, or by methods based on the Japanese practice.

My interest was first drawn in 1897 to experiments that were being made by Mr. J. D. Batten, who for two years previously had attempted, and partially succeeded in making, a print from wood and metal blocks with colour mixed with glycerine and dextrine, the glycerine being afterwards removed by washing the prints in alcohol. As the Japanese method seemed to promise greater advantages and simplicity, we began experiments together, using as our text-book the pamphlet by T. Tokuno, published by the Smithsonian Institution, Washington, and the dextrine and glycerine method was soon abandoned. The edition of prints, however, of Eve and the Serpent designed by J. D. Batten, printed by myself and published at that time, was produced partly by the earlier method and partly in the simpler Japanese way.

Familiar as everyone is with Japanese prints, it is not generally known that they are produced by means of an extremely simple craft. No machinery is required, but only a few tools for cutting the designs on the surface of the planks of cherry wood from which the impressions are taken. No press is used, but a round flat pad, which is rubbed on the back of the print as it lies on the blocks. The colours are mixed with water and paste made from rice flour. The details of the craft and photographs of the tools were given in full in the Smithsonian Institution pamphlet already mentioned.

It is slow and unsatisfactory work, however, learning manipulation from a book, and several technical difficulties that seemed insurmountable were made clear by the chance discovery in London of a Japanese printseller who, although not a printer, was sufficiently familiar with the work to give some invaluable hints and demonstrations.

Further encouragement was given to the work by the institution, a little later, of a class in wood-cuts in colour under my charge, at the L.C.C. Central School of Arts and Crafts, which for several years became the chief centre of the movement.

Such are the bare historical facts of the development in our country of this craft imported from the Far East.

On a merely superficial acquaintance the Japanese craft of block-printing may appear to be no more than a primitive though delicate form of colour reproduction, which modern mechanical methods have long superseded, even in the land of its invention; and that to study so limited a mode of expression would be hardly of any practical value to an artist. Moreover, the craft is under the disadvantage that all the stages of the work, from making the first design to taking the final impressions, must be done by the artist himself--work which includes the delicate cutting of line and planning of colour blocks, and the preparation of colour and paper. In Japan there were trained craftsmen expert in each of these branches of the craft, and each carried out his part under the supervision of the artist. No part but the design was done by him. So that the very character of the work has an essential difference. Under our present conditions the artist must undertake the whole craft, with all its detail.

Simple as the process is, there is, from first to last, a long labour involved in planning, cutting and printing, before a satisfactory batch of prints is produced. After several attempts in delegating printing to well-trained pupils I have found it impossible to obtain the best results by that means, but the cutting of the colour-blocks and the clearing of the key-block after the first cutting of the line may well be done by assistant craftsmen.

A larger demand for the prints might bring about a commercial development of the work, and the consequent employment of trained craftsmen or craftswomen, but the result would be a different one from that which has been obtained by the artists who are willing to undertake the whole production of their work.

The actual value of wood-block prints for use as decoration is a matter of personal taste and experience.

In my own opinion there is an element that always remains foreign in the prints of the Japanese masters, yet I know of no other kind of art that has the same telling value on a wall, or the same decorative charm in modern domestic rooms as the wood-block print. A single print well placed in a room of quiet colour will enrich and dominate a whole wall.

The modern vogue still favours more expensive although less decorative forms of art, or works of reproduction without colour, yet here is an art available to all who care for expressive design and colour, and within the means of the large public to whom the cost of pictures is prohibitive. In its possibility as a decorative means of expression well suited to our modern needs and uses, and in the particular charm that colour has when printed from wood on a paper that is beautiful already by its own quality, there is no doubt of the scope and opportunity offered by this art.

But as with new wine and old bottles, a new condition of simplicity in furniture and of pure colour in decoration must first be established. A wood-block print will not tell well amid a wilderness of bric-?brac or on a gaudy wall-paper.

From another and quite different point of view, the art of block-cutting and colour-printing has, however, a special and important value. To any student of pictorial art, especially to any who may wish to design for modern printed decoration, no work gives such instruction in economy of design, in the resources of line and its expressive development, and in the use and behaviour of colour. This has been the expressed opinion of many who have undertaken a course of wood-block printing for this object alone.

The same opinion is emphatically stated by Professor Emil Orlik, whose prints are well known in modern exhibitions. On the occasion of a visit to the Kunstgewerbeschule of Berlin, I found him conducting a class for designers for printed decoration, in which the Japanese craft of block-printing was made the basis of their training. He held to the view that the primitive craft teaches the students the very economy and simplicity upon which the successful use of the great modern resources of colour-printing depend, yet which cannot be learnt except by recourse to simpler conditions and more narrow limitations before dealing with the greater scope of the machine.

My own experience also convinces me that whatever may be the ultimate value of the Eastern craft to our artists as a mode of personal expression, there is no doubt of its effect and usefulness in training students to design with economy and simplicity for modern printing processes.

CHAPTER II

General Description of the Operation of Printing from a Set of Blocks

The early stages of any craft are more interesting when we are familiar with the final result. For this reason it is often an advantage to begin at the end.

To see a few impressions taken from a set of blocks in colour printing, or to print them oneself, gives the best possible idea of the quality and essential character of print-making. So also in describing the work it will perhaps tend to make the various stages clearer if the final act of printing is first explained.

The most striking characteristic of this craft is the primitive simplicity of the act of printing. No press is required, and no machinery.

A block is laid flat on the table with its cut surface uppermost, and is kept steady by a small wad of damp paper placed under each corner. A pile of paper slightly damped ready for printing lies within reach just beyond the wood-block, so that the printer may easily lift the paper sheet by sheet on to the block as it is required.

It is the practice in Japan to work squatting on the floor, with the blocks and tools also on the floor in front of the craftsman. Our own habit of working at a table is less simple, but has some advantages. One practice or habit of the Japanese is, however, to be followed with particular care. No description can give quite fully the sense of extreme orderliness and careful deliberation of their work. Everything is placed where it will be most convenient for use, and this orderliness is preserved throughout the day's work. Their shapely tools and vessels are handled with a deftness that shames our clumsy ways, and everything that they use is kept quite clean. This skilful orderliness is essential to fine craftmanship, and is a sign of mastery.

When printing on a table arranged in this way the board lying on the sheets of damped paper at B is first lifted off and placed at C to receive the sheets as they are done. If the block A is quite dry, it is thoroughly moistened with a damp sponge and wiped. The colour from a saucer, E, is then brushed over the printing surface thinly, and a trace of paste taken from F is also brushed into the colour. (This is best done after the colour is roughly spread on the block.) The brush is laid down in its place, D, and the top sheet of paper from the pile is immediately lifted to its register marks (notches to keep the paper in its place) on the block. The manner of holding the paper is shown on page

70. This must be done deftly, and it is important to waste no time, as the colour would soon dry on the exposed block and print badly.

Pressure is then applied to the back of the paper as it lies on the wet block. This is done by a round pad called the baren by the Japanese. It is made of a coil of cord covered by bamboo sheath as shown later on page 62. The pad is rubbed by hand with considerable pressure, moving transversely forwards and backwards across the block, working from the left to the right. Once all over the block should be enough. The paper is then lifted off and laid face upwards on the board at C. The block is then re-charged with colour for another impression, and the whole operation repeated as many times as there are sheets to be printed.

When this is done all the sheets will have received a single impression, which may be either a patch of colour or an impression in line of part of the design of the print. The block A is then removed, cleaned, and put away; and the block for the second impression put in its place.

It is usual to print the line or key-block of a design first, as one is then able to detect faulty registering or imperfect fitting of the blocks and to correct them at once. But there are cases in which a gradated tone, such as a sky, may need to be printed before the line block.

The complete design of a print may require several blocks for colour as well as the key block which prints the line. The impressions from all these blocks may be printed one after another without waiting for the colour on the paper to dry.

As soon as the batch of damped sheets has been passed over the first block, the sheets are replaced at B between boards, and, if necessary, damped again by means of damping sheets (as described later in Chapter V) ready for the next impression, which may be proceeded with at once without fear of the colour running. It is a remarkable fact that patches of wet colour which touch one another do not run if properly printed.

For the second printing fresh colour is prepared and clean paste, and the printing proceeds as already described, care being taken to watch the proper registering or fitting of each impression to its place in the design.

There are many niceties and details to be observed in the printing of both line and colour blocks. These are given in special chapters following. This description of the main action of printing will be of use in giving a general idea of the final operation before the details of the preliminary stages are described.

CHAPTER III

Description of the Materials and Tools required for Block-cutting

The wood most commonly used by the Japanese for their printing-blocks is a cherry wood very similar to that grown in England. The Canadian cherry wood, which is more easily obtained than English cherry, is of too open a grain to be of use. The more slowly grown English wood has a closer grain and is the best for all the purposes of block cutting and printing. Well-seasoned planks should be obtained and kept ready for cutting up as may be required.

When a set of blocks is to be cut for a given design, the size of the printing surface of each block should be made equal to the size of the design plus 1 inch or, for large prints, 1-1/2 inch in addition long ways, and 1/4 or 1/2 inch crossways. The thickness of the plank need not be more than 5/8 or 3/4 inch. It is best for the protection of the surfaces of the printing blocks and to prevent warping, also for convenience in storing and handling them, to fix across each end a piece of wood slightly thicker than the plank itself. .

Both surfaces of the plank should be planed smooth and then finished with a steel scraper, but not touched with sand-paper.

It is understood that the face of the plank is used for the printing surface, and not the end of the grain as in blocks for modern wood engraving.

The tools needed for cutting the blocks are the following:

## 1. THE KNIFE

With this knife the most important and delicate work is done. All the lines of the key-block as well as the boundaries of the colour masses are cut with it, before the removal of intervening spaces.

The blade lies in a slot and is held tight by the tapered ferrule. This can be pulled off by hand and the blade lengthened by pulling it forward in the slot.

## 2. CHISELS

These are used for removing the wood between the cut lines or colour masses, and should be ordinary carvers' chisels of the following sizes except those under No. 9, which are short-handled chisels for small work.

The Japanese toolmakers fit these small chisels into a split handle as shown in fig. 5. The blade is held tightly in its place by the tapered ferrule when the handle is closed, or can be lengthened by opening the handle and pulling forward the blade in its slot. In this way the blade can be used down to its last inch.

## 3. MALLET

This is needed for driving the larger chisels.

These are all the tools that are needed for block cutting. For keeping them in order it is well to have oilstones of three grades:

1. A carborundum stone for rapidly re-covering the shape of a chipped or blunt tool.

2. A good ordinary oil stone.

3. A hard stone for keeping a fine edge on the knife in cutting line blocks. The American "Washita" stone is good for this purpose.

CHAPTER IV

Block Cutting and the Planning of Blocks

The cutting of a line block needs patience and care and skill, but it is not the most difficult part of print making, nor is it so hopeless an enterprise as it seems at first to one who has not tried to use the block-cutter's knife.

In Japan this work is a highly specialised craft, never undertaken by the artist himself, but carried out by skilled craftsmen who only do this part of the work of making colour prints. Even the clearing of the spaces between the cut lines is done by assistant craftsmen or craftswomen.

The exquisite perfection of the cutting of the lines in the finest of the Japanese prints, as, for instance, the profile of a face in a design by Outamaro, has required the special training and tradition of generations of craftsmen.

The knife, however, is not a difficult weapon to an artist who has hands and a trained sense of form. In carrying out his own work, moreover, he may express a quality that is of greater value even than technical perfection.

At present we have no craftsmen ready for this work--nor could our designs be safely trusted to the interpretation of Japanese block-cutters. Until we train craftsmen among ourselves we must therefore continue to cut our own blocks.

CUTTING

A set of blocks consists of a key-block and several colour blocks. The block that must be cut first is that which prints the line or "key" of the design. By means of impressions from this key-block the various other blocks for printing the coloured portions of the design are cut. The key-block is the most important of the set of blocks and contains the essential part of the design.

A drawing of that part of the design which is to be cut on the key-block should first be made. This is done on the thinnest of Japanese tissue paper in black indelible ink. The drawing is then pasted face downward on the prepared first block with good starch paste. It is best to lay the drawing flat on its back upon a pad of a few sheets of paper of about the same size, and to rub the paste on the surface of the block, not on the paper. The block is now laid down firmly with its pasted side on the drawing, which at once adheres to the block. Next turn the block over and lay a dry sheet of paper over the damp drawing so as to protect it, and with the baren, or printing rubber, rub the drawing flat, and well on to the block all over.

The drawing should then be allowed to dry thoroughly on the block.

With regard to the design of the key block, it is a common mistake to treat this as a drawing only of outlines of the forms of the print. Much modern so-called decorative printing has been weak in this respect. A flat, characterless line, with no more expression than a bent gaspipe, is often printed round the forms of a design, followed by printings of flat colour, the whole resulting in a travesty of "flat" decorative treatment.

The key design should be a skeleton of all the forms of a print, expressing much more than mere exterior boundaries. It may so suggest form that although the colour be printed by a flat tint the result is not flat. When one is unconscious of any flatness in the final effect, though the result is obtained by flat printing, then the proper use of flat treatment has been made. The affectation of flatness in inferior colour printing and poster work is due to a misapprehension of the true principle of flat treatment.

As an illustration of the great variety of form that may be expressed by the key-block, a reproduction is given (page 33) of an impression from a Japanese key-block. It will be seen that the lines and spots express much more than boundaries of form. In the case of the lighter tree foliage the boundaries are left to be determined entirely by the subsequent colour blocks, and only the interior form or character of the foliage is suggested. The quality or kind of line, too, varies with the thing expressed, whether tree, rock, sea, or the little ship. The design, too, is in itself beautiful and gives the essential form of the entire print.

The study of the drawing of any of the key-blocks of the Japanese masters will reveal their wonderful power and resource in the suggestion of essential form by black lines, spots, and masses of one uniform tint of black or grey. The development of this kind of expressive drawing is most important to the designer of printed decoration, whether by wood blocks, or lithography, or any other printing process.

Other good types of drawing for the purposes of key-blocks in wood are given on Plate V facing page 26 and Plate XVI p. iii in Appendix.

When the key-block with its design pasted upon it is thoroughly dry, a little sweet oil should be rubbed with the finger at that part where the cutting is to begin, so as to make the paper transparent and the black line quite clear.

In order to keep the block from moving on the work-table, there should be fixed one or two strips of wood screwed down, to act as stops in case the block tends to slip, but the block should lie freely on the table, so that it may be easily turned round during the cutting when necessary. One should, however, learn to use the cutting knife in all directions, and to move the block as little as possible.

The knife is held and guided by the right hand, but is pushed along by the middle finger of the left hand placed at the back of the blade, close down near the point. The left hand should be generally flat on the work-table, palm down, and the nail of the middle finger must be kept short. This position is shown (fig. 7) on p. 30.

The flat side of the knife should always be against the line to be cut.

Sometimes it is convenient to drive the knife from right to left, but in this case the pressure is given by the right hand, and the left middle finger is used to check and steady the knife, the finger being pressed against the knife just above the cutting edge.

A good position for cutting a long straight line towards oneself on the block is shown below (fig. 8). The left hand is on its side, and the middle finger is hooked round and pulls the knife while the right hand guides it.

In all cases the middle finger of the left hand pushes or steadies the knife, or acts as a fulcrum.

A beginner with the knife usually applies too much pressure or is apt to put the left finger at a point too high up on the blade, where it loses its control. The finger should be as close down to the wood as possible, where its control is most effective. A small piece of india-rubber tubing round the knife blade helps to protect the finger.

With practice the knife soon becomes an easy and a very precise tool, capable of great expressiveness in drawing. Bear in mind that both sides of a line are drawn by the knife. The special power of developing the expressive form of line on both sides is a resource tending to great development of drawing in designs for wood-block prints. The line may be of varying form, changing from silhouette to pure line as may best serve to express the design. It should never be a mere diagram.

The actual cutting proceeds as follows: Starting at some point where the surface of the key-block design has been oiled and made distinct, a shallow cut is made along one side of any form in the design, with the knife held slanting so that the cut slants away from the edge of the form. A second outer parallel cut is then made with the knife held slanting in the opposite direction from the first, so that the two cuts together make a V-shaped trench all along the line of the form. The little strip of wood cut out should detach itself as the second cut is made, and should not need any picking out or further cutting if the first two cuts are cleanly made. This shallow V-shaped trench is continued all round the masses and along both sides of all the lines of the design. No clearing of the intervening spaces should be attempted until this is done. It will be seen at once that the V-shaped cuts give great strength to the printing lines, so that a quite fine line between two cuts may have a strong, broad base (fig. 9). The depth of the cut would be slightly shallower than that shown in this diagram. In cutting fine line work a cut is first made a little beyond the line, then the cut is made on the line itself (fig. 10).

Where a very fine line is to be cut, especially if it is on a curve, the outer cut of the V trench should be made first, and then that which touches the line: there is thus less disturbance of the wood, and less danger of injuring the edge of the line.

When the V cut has been made outside all the lines, one proceeds to clear the intervening spaces between the lines of the design by taking tool No. 1 (fig. 5). The large spaces should be cleared first. The safest and quickest way is to make a small gouge cut with No. 1 round all the large spaces close up to the first cut, then, with one of the shallower chisels, Nos. 5, 6, or 7 (fig. 5), and the mallet, clear out the wood between the gouge cuts.

For all shallow cuts where the mallet is not needed, the Japanese hold the chisels as shown in fig. 11. With practice this will be found a very convenient and steady grip for the right hand. It has also the advantage that the chisel can be held against the centre of the body and exactly under one's eyes.

In the diagram (fig. 12), if the wood from A to A1 is to be cleared away, gouge cuts are made at b and b1, then the space between b and b1 may be quickly cleared without risk to the edge of the form at A. When this rough work is done the little ridge between A and b may be cleared with small round or flat tools, as is most convenient. But this final clearing should not be done until all the large spaces are roughed out.

The depth to which the spaces must be cleared will depend on their width, as, in printing, the paper will sag more deeply in a wide space than in a narrow one. In spaces of half an inch the depth of the first V-cuts is sufficient, but the proportionate depth is about that of the diagram above. The small spaces are cleared by means of small flat or round chisels without the mallet or the preliminary gouge cut: this is only needed where a large space has to be cleared.

There remain now only the placing and cutting of the two register marks or notches for controlling the position of the paper in printing.

These are placed relatively to the design as shown in fig. 13.

The corner of the print fits into the notch at A, and one edge of the print lies against the straight notch at B.

The register marks may be even closer to the space covered by the design, but must not actually touch it, as some margin of paper is necessary in printing: they should also be cut always on the long side of the printing block. It will be seen from the drawing on page 70 that these register marks correspond to the position of the thumb of each hand in laying the paper on the block for printing.

The corner mark, ABC, is made by cutting from A to B and B to C, with the knife held perpendicularly, and its flat side against the line, then the shaded portion is cut with a flat chisel, sloping from the surface of the block at AC to a depth of about 1/16 inch along AB and BC. The straight notch, EF, is similarly cut, first with a perpendicular knife along EF, and then the shaded portion is chiselled sloping down to the line EF.

In section the two register marks would be as above.

The register marks must be smoothly and evenly cut so that the paper, in printing, may slide easily home to its exact place.

When the design of the key-block and the two register marks have been cut and cleared, the trace of paper and paste on the uncut parts of the wood should be carefully washed off with a piece of sponge and warm water. The block is then finished and ready for use. The key-block, however, is only one of the set of blocks required for a print in colour, but the colour blocks are simpler and require, as a rule, far less labour.

The colour blocks are planned and established by means of impressions taken from the key-block. For this purpose the register marks are inked[2] for printing as well as the design on the block, and the impressions must include both. These impressions are taken on thin Japanese paper, but not necessarily the thinnest tissue. If the thinnest is used, it should be pasted at the corners to a sheet of stiffer paper for convenience in handling.

[2] The preparation of the ink for printing is described on p. 54.

It is then a fairly simple matter to take one of these key-block impressions and to make a plan of the various colour-blocks that will be required. These should obviously be as few as possible.

It is not necessary to provide an entire block for each patch of colour, but only the extent of surface required for each coloured portion of the print, as well as for its pair of register marks. Patches of different colour that are not adjacent to one another on the design of the print may be cut on the same block, provided they are not too close for free colouring of the block in printing. Each block also may be cut on both sides, so that there is considerable scope for economy in the arranging and planning of the colour blocks.

When the arrangement of the plan of colour has been simplified as far as possible, a new block is prepared as described above, and a sheet of thin Japanese paper (unsized) is cut large enough to cover the print design and its register marks. The clean surface of the new block is covered thinly with starch paste well rubbed into the grain, and while this is still wet an impression on the sheet of thin Japanese paper is taken of the entire key-block, including its register marks in black, and laid before it is dry face downward on the pasted surface of the new block. This should be done as already described on page 25. It should be rubbed flat with the printing pad and left to dry.

This operation requires careful handling, but it should be done easily and methodically, without any hurry.

Each side of the set of colour planks should be treated in the same way--a thin impression of the key-block and its register marks being laid upon each. It is advisable to paste down a freshly taken impression, each time, while the ink is still moist, for if these are allowed to dry, the shrinking of the paper causes errors of register.

When these new blocks are dry, the patch of colour to be cut on each surface should be clearly indicated by a thin wash of diluted ink or colour, but not so as to hide the printed key line.

The blocks may then be cut. A V-shaped cut is made round each form, as in the case of the key-block, and the clearing proceeds in the same way, but it is only necessary to clear a space of about an inch round each form: the rest of the wood should be left standing. A section of the printing surface of a colour block would be as follows:

When the register marks corresponding to these colour forms have also been cut, and the paper washed off the blocks, the clear spaces may be used for pasting down new key impressions for the smaller colour patches and their corresponding register marks. In this way one side of a colour plank may contain several different colour forms and sets of register marks. As a rule the different colour patches would be printed separately, though in some cases two colours may be printed at one impression if they are small and have the same register marks.

When the blocks have been cut and cleared it is advisable to smooth with sand-paper the edge of the depression where it meets the uncut surface of the wood, otherwise this edge, if at all sharp, will mark the print.

For any particulars about which one may be in doubt, the sets of blocks at South Kensington Museum or in the Print Room at the British Museum are available for examination. In one of the sets at the British Museum it is interesting to see the temporary corrections that have been made in the register marks during printing by means of little wooden plugs stuck into the register notches.

In nearly all cases the Japanese blocks were made of cherry wood, but planks of box are said to have been occasionally used for very fine work.

ERRORS OF REGISTER

However exactly the register marks may be cut in a new set of blocks, very puzzling errors occasionally arise while printing, especially if the planks are of thin wood.

Some of the blocks are necessarily printed drier than others. For instance, the key-block is printed with a very small amount of ink and paste. Other blocks may be even drier, such as the blocks which print small forms or details in a design. The blocks, however, which are used for large masses of colour, or for gradated tones, are moistened over the whole or a large part of the surface of the block, and if the wood is thin, and not well mounted across the ends, the block soon expands sufficiently to throw the register out. If the block is not mounted across the ends there will also be a tendency to warp, and this will add to the errors of register. But if the blocks are of fairly thick wood, and well mounted, the register will remain very exact indeed.

Usually the key-block is printed first. If the subsequent blocks are not in exact register the error is noticeable at once, and slight adjustments may be made for its correction. But in cases where the key-block is printed last (as sometimes is necessary) each colour block must be tested before a batch of prints is passed over it. For this purpose the first few prints of every batch should receive a faint impression of the key-block, so that the register of the colour impression may be verified before proceeding with the whole batch.

If these precautions are taken, and the entire set of blocks kept as nearly as possible in the same conditions of dryness or moisture, all difficulties of register in printing will be easily overcome.

When cutting a new set of blocks there is another possible source of error which needs to be carefully guarded against. Most of the work in designing a new print is necessarily spent in planning and cutting the key-block, which may occupy a considerable time, especially if other work has to be carried on as well. If new wood is used, or wood that has not been seasoned long indoors, it will dry and contract considerably across the grain before the work is finished. Then, if newer planks are prepared and cut up for the colour blocks, and impressions from the key-block are pasted down on them for cutting, it will be found that, as the newer wood of the colour-blocks goes on drying, it will shrink out of register, and the colour impressions will not fit the line perfectly. It is easy to fall into this difficulty, but there is no danger of it if the planks from which the key-block and the colour-blocks are cut are all equally seasoned and are in the same condition.

CHAPTER V

Preparation of Paper, Ink, Colour, and Paste for Printing

PAPER

The paper made by the Japanese from the inner bark of young shoots of the mulberry and certain other plants of similar fibre is beyond all others the best for wood-block printing. It is in itself a very remarkable material, and is used in Japan for a great variety of purposes, on account of the strength and toughness due to its long silky fibre.

Paper of good quality for printing may be obtained directly from Japan, or through trading agents dealing with Japan. A case of five reams would be the smallest quantity obtainable directly, but it is by far the cheapest and most satisfactory way of buying it. In smaller quantities the paper is obtainable through many of the dealers in artists' materials. Several kinds of this paper are made, but unsized sheets of a quality similar to the print on page 95, and a thin Japanese tissue paper are the two kinds required for printing in colour.

In its unsized state the paper is too absorbent for use, and it should be sized freshly as needed for work. This is done by brushing a thin solution of gelatine over the smooth surface of the sheets of paper.

A drawing-board rather larger than the sheets of paper, placed as shown in fig. 17, with its lower edge resting on a basin of warm size, will be found a convenient arrangement.

(To face page 48.)]

The sheet gelatine sold by grocers for cooking makes an excellent size. Six of the thin sheets to a pint of water is a good strength.[3] The gelatine is dissolved in hot water, but should not be boiled, as that partially destroys the size. When dissolved, a little powdered alum is also stirred in, about as much as will lie on a shilling to a pint of water. The addition of the alum is important, as it acts as a mordant and helps to make a better colour impression.

[3] See also p. 75.

In applying the size to the paper a four-inch broad flat paste brush is used. The paper is laid on the slanting board and the size brushed backward and forward across the paper from the upper end downward. Care must be taken not to make creases in the paper, as these become permanent. To avoid this the lower end of the sheet may be held with the left hand and raised when necessary as the brush passes downwards. The waste size will run down to the basin, but the paper need not be flooded, nor should its surface be brushed unnecessarily, but it must be fully and evenly charged with size. The sheet is then picked up by the two upper corners (which may conveniently be kept unsized) and pinned at each corner over a cord stretched across the workroom. The sheets are left hanging until they are dry. The Japanese lay the paper on the cord, letting the two halves of the sheet hang down equally on either side.

The process of sizing and drying the sheets of paper is illustrated in a print shown in the collection at the South Kensington Museum.

When the paper is quite dry it is taken down, and if required at once for printing should be cut up into sheets of the size required, with sufficient margin allowed to reach the register marks. It is best to cut a gauge or pattern in cardboard for use in cutting the sheets to a uniform size.

A few sheets of unsized paper are needed as damping sheets, one being used to every three printing sheets. The damping sheets should be cut at least an inch wider and longer than the printing sheets. Two wooden boards are also required. The sheets of printing paper are kept between these while damping before work.

To prepare for work, a damping sheet is taken and brushed over evenly with water with a broad brush (like that used for sizing). The sheet must not be soaked, but made thoroughly moist, evenly all over. It is then laid on one of the two boards, and on it, with the printing side (the smoother side) downward, are laid three of the sized sheets of printing paper. On these another moist damping sheet is laid, and again three dry sheets of printing paper, face downwards, and so on alternately to the number of sheets of the batch to be printed. A board is placed on the top of the pile.

The number of prints to be attempted at one printing will vary with the kind of work and with the printer's experience. The printing may be continued during three days, but if the paper is kept damp longer, there is danger of mould and spotting. With work requiring delicate gradation of colour and many separate block impressions twenty or thirty sheets will be found sufficient for three days' hard work. The professional printers of Japan, however, print batches of two hundred and three hundred prints at a time, but in that case the work must become largely mechanical.[4]

[4] See Chapter XIII for further experience on this point.

The batch of paper and damping sheets should remain between the boards for at least half an hour when new sheets are being damped for the first time. The damping sheets, all but the top and bottom ones, should then be removed and the printing sheets left together between the boards for some time before printing. An hour improves their condition very much, the moisture spreading equally throughout the batch of sheets. Before printing they should be quite flat and soft, but scarcely moist to the touch. If the sheets are new, they may even be left standing all night after the first damping, and will be in perfect condition for printing in the morning without further damping. No weight should be placed on the boards.

Although no paper has hitherto been found that will take so perfect an impression from colour-blocks as the long-fibred Japanese paper, yet it should be the aim of all craftsmen to become independent of foreign materials as far as possible. There is no doubt that our paper-makers should be able to produce a paper of good quality sufficiently absorbent to take colour from the wet block and yet tough enough to bear handling when slightly damp.

If a short-fibred paper is made without size, it comes to pieces when it is damped for printing. But the amount of absorbency required is not so great as to preclude the use of size altogether. It is a problem which our paper-makers could surely solve. A soft, slightly absorbent, white paper is required. At present nothing has been produced to take the place of the long mulberry fibre of the Japanese, which prints perfectly, but it is far from being pure white in colour. A white paper would have a great advantage in printing high and delicate colour schemes.

INK

Next in importance is the preparation of the ink for printing the key-block or any black or grey parts of a design. As a rule the key-block is printed black, more or less diluted with paste; indeed the key-block is often printed very faintly by means of paste only just tinged with a trace of black.

The use of colour for the key-block is treated in Chapter VII. The ink is prepared as follows. Take a stick of solid Chinese ink of good quality, and break it with a hammer into fragments; put these to soak in a pot with water for three or four days. (The quality of the sticks of Chinese ink varies greatly. The cheap sticks make a coarse and gritty ink which does not print well.) Day by day pour off the water, adding fresh, so that the glue that soaks out of the softened black fragments is removed. Three days is usually long enough for this. If left too long the whole mass goes bad and is spoiled. When the black mass is soft and clean drain off the water and rub the ink smooth in a dish with a bone palette knife. It is then ready for use, but would rapidly go bad if not used up at once, so that a preservative is necessary to keep a stock of ink in good condition. An effective method is to put the ink at once into a well-corked, wide-mouthed bottle. To the under side of the cork is nailed a little wad of unsized paper soaked with creosote. By this means ink can be kept in perfect condition for weeks or months. A drop of fresh creosote should occasionally be put on the wad fixed to the cork.

Fresh ink may at any time be obtained rapidly in small quantities by rubbing down a stick of Chinese ink on a slab in the ordinary way, but this is very laborious, and is only worth while if one needs a small quantity of a glossy black, for which the rubbed-down ink containing all its glue is the best.

COLOUR

Any colour that can be obtained in a fine dry powder may be used in wood-block printing. Some artists have succeeded in using ordinary water colours sold in tubes, by mixing the colour with the rice paste before printing; but the best results are obtained by the use of pure, finely ground dry colour mixed only with water, the rice paste being added actually on the block.

Most of the artists' colour merchants supply colour by weight in the form of dry powder: any colour that is commonly used in oil or water-colour painting may be obtained in this state. A stock of useful colours should be kept in wide-necked bottles.

A few shallow plates or small dishes are needed to hold colour and a bone or horn palette knife for mixing and rubbing the colour into a smooth paste in the dishes. Small bone paper knives are useful for taking colour from the bottles.

When the colour scheme of a print is made certain--and this is best done by printing small experimental batches--it is a good plan to have a number of covered pots equal to the number of the different colour impressions, and to fill these with a quantity of each tint, the colour or colours being mixed smoothly with water to the consistency of stiff cream.

Some colours will be found to print more smoothly and easily than others. Yellow ochre, for instance, prints with perfect smoothness and ease, while heavier or more gritty colours tend to separate and are more difficult. In the case of a very heavy colour such as vermilion, a drop of glue solution will keep the colour smooth for printing, and less paste is necessary. But most colours will give good impressions by means of rice paste alone. It is essential, however, that only very finely ground colours of good quality should be used.

PASTE

A paste must be used with the colour in order to hold it on to the surface of the paper and to give brilliancy. The colour, if printed without paste, would dry to powder again. The paste also preserves the matt quality which is characteristic of the Japanese prints.

Finely ground rice flour may be obtained from grocery dealers. An excellent French preparation of rice sold in packets as Cr 阮 e de Riz is perfect for the purpose of making paste for printing. It should be carefully made as follows: While half a pint of water is put to boil in a saucepan over a small spirit lamp or gas burner, mix in a cup about two teaspoonfuls of rice flour with water, added little by little until a smooth cream is made with no lumps in it. A bone spoon is good for this purpose. Pour this mixture into the boiling water in the saucepan all at once, and stir well till it boils again, after which it should be left simmering over a small flame for five minutes.

When the paste has cooled it should be smooth and almost fluid enough to pour: not stiff like a pudding.

While printing, a little paste is put out in a saucer and replenished from time to time.

Fresh paste should be made every day.

CHAPTER VI

Detailed Method of Printing

Success in printing depends very much on care and orderliness. It is necessary to keep to a fixed arrangement of the position of everything on the work-table and to have all kept as clean as possible. To see the deft and unhurried work of a Japanese craftsman at printing is a great lesson, and a reproach to Western clumsiness.

The positions indicated by the diagram on page 11 will be found to be practical and convenient.

The special tools used in printing are the "baren" or printing pad, which is the only instrument of pressure used, and the printing brushes.

THE BAREN OR PRINTING PAD

As made by the Japanese, the baren is about five inches in diameter, and consists of a circular board upon which a flat coil of cord or twisted fibre is laid. This is held in place by a covering made of a strip of bamboo-sheath, the two ends of which are twisted and brought together at the back of the board so as to form a handle. The flat surface of the bamboo-sheath is on the under side of the pad when the handle is uppermost. The ribbed bamboo-sheath is impervious to the dampness of the paper in printing, and the pad may be used to rub and press directly on the back of the damp paper as it lies on the block without any protective backing sheet. The collotype reproduction facing page 12 shows the shape and character of the baren.

Japanese printing pads may be obtained from some of the artists' colour-men, or from Japan through various agencies. They are by far the best instrument for the purpose. A pad lasts a considerable time, and when the bamboo sheath wears through may be re-covered as described below. If the new bamboo sheath is unobtainable, the baren may be re-covered by a sheet of vegetable parchment (of the kind used for covering pots of jam), laid on when wet, and twisted and bound at the end like the original bamboo covering. A baren used and re-covered when worn will last for an indefinite time in this way.

TO RE-COVER A WORN BAREN WITH BAMBOO SHEATH

Damp the new leaf in water with a brush on both sides thoroughly.

Wipe dry both sides. Lay it on a flat surface and stretch wider with the fingers on the inside, keeping the leaf flat with the palm of the hand.

Rub the inside of the leaf with something hard and smooth across the width on both sides.

1. Cut AG, BG with leaf folded.

2. Place the round pad in position on the flat leaf.

3. Stretch the leaf to lap at sides EF.

4. Turn in EA and BF fold by fold, first one side and then the other.

5. Pull hard before beginning the other end.

6. Cut away CH, DH, holding down firmly the end done.

7. Twist up the ends tightly, pull over to the centre, and tie tightly together; cut off ends.

8. Polish on board and oil slightly.

Twist the inside part of the baren occasionally to save wear by changing its position within the sheath.

Several substitutes have been tried in place of the Japanese baren, with coverings of leather, shark's skin, celluloid, and various other materials, but these necessitate the use of a backing sheet to protect the paper from their harsh surfaces.

An ingenious rubber of ribbed glass which works directly on the paper has been devised by Mr. William Giles, who has produced beautiful results by its means.

If one is using the Japanese baren, its surface needs to be kept very slightly oiled to enable it to run freely over the damp paper. A pad of paper with a drop of sweet oil suffices for this, and may lie on the right of the printing block where the baren is put after each impression is taken.

An even simpler method is that of the Japanese craftsman who rubs the baren from time to time on the back of his head.

BRUSHES

Japanese printing brushes are sold by some artists' colour dealers, but these are not essential, nor have they any practical superiority over well-made Western brushes.

An excellent type of brush is that made of black Siberian bear hair for fine varnishing. These can be had from good brush-makers with the hair fixed so that it will stand soaking in water. Drawings of the type of brush are given above.

Three or four are sufficient; one broad brush, about three inches, for large spaces, one two-inch, and two one-inch, will do nearly all that is needed. Occasionally a smaller brush may be of use.

PRINTING

To begin printing, one takes first the key-block, laying it upon a wet sheet of unsized paper, or upon wads of wet paper under each corner of the block, which will keep it quite steady on the work-table. A batch of sheets of printing paper, prepared and damped as described in Chapter V, lies between boards just beyond the block. The pad lies close to the block at the right on oily paper pinned to the table. To the right also are a dish or plate on which a little ink is spread, the printing brush (broad for the key-block), a saucer containing fresh paste, a bowl of water, a small sponge, and a cloth. Nothing else is needed, and it is best to keep the table clear of unnecessary pots or colour bottles.

When these things are ready one should see that the paper is in a good state. It should be rather drier for a key-block than for other blocks, as a fine line will print thickly if the paper is too damp and soft. In fact, it can scarcely be too dry for the key-block, provided that it has become perfectly smooth, and is still flexible enough for complete contact with the block. But it must not be either dry or damp in patches.

If the paper is all right, one lifts off the upper board and top damping sheet, placing them on the left, ready to receive the sheets when printed.

The key-block, if quite dry, must be moistened with a damp sponge and then brushed over with the broad printing brush and ink. If a grey line is wanted the brush should be dipped in a little of the paste and scarcely touched with ink. For a pale grey line the key-block also must be well washed before printing. Even if the line is to be black a little paste should be used. This is best added after one has brushed the black ink on to the block, not mixed with it beforehand. The ink and paste are then broken together smoothly and completely over the whole surface of the block. The last few brush strokes should be of the full length or breadth of the block and be given lightly with the brush held upright. The inking of the block must be thoroughly done, but with no more brushing than is necessary to spread the colour equally. When properly charged with ink the block should not be at all wet, but just covered with a very thin and nearly dry film of ink and paste.

No time should be wasted in lifting the top sheet of printing paper on to the block, placing first its right corner in the register notch, and holding it there with the thumb, then the edge of the paper to the other notch, to be held with the left thumb while the right hand is released to take up the baren (fig. 21). Beginning at the left, the baren is rubbed backwards and forwards, a full stroke each time, to the outside limits of the block, with a moderate, even pressure, moving the stroke in a zigzag towards the right end of the block (fig. 22). Once over should be enough. A second rub makes heavy printing of the finer lines. Then the paper is lifted from the block and placed on the board to the left.

Particular attention must be given to the careful placing of the paper home in the register notches, and to holding it there until the rubber has gripped the paper on the block.

Sheet by sheet all the printing paper is passed in this way over the key-block, and piled together. There is no fear of the ink offsetting or marking the print placed above it. As the work proceeds the block will give better and better impressions. Spoiled or defective impressions should be put together at the top of the pile when it lies ready for the next printing, for the first few impressions are always uncertain, and it is well to use the defective prints as pioneers, so as not to spoil good ones.

When the block has been printed on the whole batch, the sheets should be replaced at once between the boards before one prepares for the colour impressions. Usually the paper will be too dry for colour by this time: if this is so, the damping sheets should be moistened and put in again as before; one to each three printing sheets. In a minute or two they will have damped the paper sufficiently and must be taken out, leaving the printing sheets to stand, between the boards, ready for the first colour-block.

PRINTING FROM COLOUR-BLOCKS

In printing colour the paper may be slightly damper than it should be for key-block impressions, and a heavier pressure is necessary on the baren if the colour masses are large. If the baren is pressed lightly the colour will not completely cover the paper, but will leave a dry, granular texture. Occasionally this quality may be useful, but as a rule a smooth, evenly printed surface is best. It will be found that smooth, even printing is not obtained by loading the block with colour or paste, but by using the least possible quantity of both, and nearly dry paper.

In beginning to print from a colour-block, care should be taken to moisten the block fully before printing, or it will not yield the colour from its surface; but the block must be wiped, and not used while actually wet.

The printing proceeds exactly as in the case of the key-block, except for the heavier use of the baren. The paste should be added after the colour has been roughly brushed on to the block, and then the two are smoothly brushed together. The Japanese printers put the paste on to the block by means of a little stick kept in the dish of paste. Experience will soon show the amount of paste needed. It is important neither to add too much nor to stint the paste, as the colour when dry depends on the paste for its quality. Too little paste gives a dead effect.

Some of the colours print more easily than others. With a sticky colour it is well to wipe the block with a nearly dry sponge between each impression, so that the wood gives up its colour more readily. In the case of a very heavy colour such as vermilion a drop of glue and water may help; but with practically all the colours that are generally used the rice paste and careful printing are enough.

The amount of size in the paper is another important factor in the printing of colour. If the paper is too lightly sized the fibres will detach themselves and stick to the damp block. Or if too heavily sized the paper will not take up the colour cleanly from the block, and will look hard when dry. One very soon feels instinctively the right quality and condition of the block, colour, and paper which are essential to good printing; and to print well one must become sensitive to them.

PRINTING OF GRADATIONS

Beside the printing of flat masses of colour, one of the great resources of block printing is in the power of delicate gradation in printing. The simplest way of making a gradation from strong to pale colour is to dip one corner of a broad brush into the colour and the other corner into water so that the water just runs into the colour: then, by squeezing the whole width of the brush broadly between the thumb and forefinger so that most of the water is squeezed out, the brush is left charged with a tint gradated from side to side. The brush is then dipped lightly into paste along its whole edge, and brushed a few times to and fro across the block where the gradation is needed. It is easy in this way to print a very delicately gradated tint from full colour to white. If the pale edge of the tint is to disappear, the block should be moistened along the surface with a sponge where the colour is to cease.

A soft edge may be given to a tint with a brush ordinarily charged if the block is moistened with a clean sponge at the part where the tint is to cease. This effect is often seen at the top of the sky in a Japanese landscape print where a dark blue band of colour is printed with a soft edge suddenly gradated to white, or sometimes the plumage of birds is printed with sudden gradations. In fact, the method may be developed in all kinds of ways. Often it is an advantage to print a gradation and then a flat tone over the gradation in a second printing.

OFFSETTING

No care need be taken to prevent "offsetting" of the colour while printing. The prints may be piled on the top of each other immediately as they are lifted from the block, without fear of offsetting or marking each other. Only an excessive use of colour, or the leaving of heavy ridges of colour at the edges of the block by careless brushing, will sometimes mark the next print on the pile. As in printing the key-block, it is well to hold the brush quite upright for the last strokes across the block, and always to give a full stroke across the whole length or width of the form to be coloured.

As soon as one colour-block has been printed, the next may be taken and printed at once, without fear of the colour running, even though the fresh colour touches the parts already printed.

One by one each colour-block is printed in this way until the batch of paper has been passed over the whole set of blocks composing the design of the print. There may sometimes be an advantage in not printing the key-block first, though as a rule it should come first for the sake of keeping the later blocks in proper register. If the key-block is not printed one cannot see how the colour-blocks are fitting. But in the case of a sky with perhaps two or even three printings--a gradation and a flat tone or two gradations--there is danger of blurring the lines of the key-block, so that in such a case the sky should be printed first, and then the key-block followed by the remaining colour-blocks.

At the end of a day's printing the prints may quite safely be left standing together between the boards until the next day. For three days the damp paper comes to no harm, except in hot weather, but on the fourth day little red spots of mould begin to show and spread. It should be remembered that freshly boiled paste is to be used each day.

DRYING OF PRINTS

When the prints are finished they should be put to dry as soon as possible. If they are spread out and left exposed to the air they will soon dry, but in drying will cockle, and cannot then be easily pressed flat. It is better to have a number of mill-boards or absorbent "pulp" boards rather larger than the prints, and to pile the prints and boards alternately one by one, placing a weight on the top of the pile. The absorbent boards will rapidly dry the prints and keep them quite flat.

Finished prints should be numbered for reference, and should, if printed by the artist himself, also bear his signature --or some printed sign to that effect. The number of prints obtainable from a set of blocks is difficult to estimate. The Japanese printers are said to have made editions of several thousands from single sets of blocks. The actual wear in printing even of a fine line block is imperceptible, for the pressure is very slight. Certainly hundreds of prints can be made without any deterioration. But an artist who is both designing and producing his own work will not be inclined to print large editions.[5]

[5] Further experience on this point is given in Chapter VIII on Co-operative Printing.

CHAPTER VII

Principles and Main Considerations in designing Wood-block Prints--Their Application to Modern Colour Printing

Until one has become quite familiar with the craft of wood-block printing it is not possible to make a satisfactory design for a print, or to understand either the full resources that are available or the limits that are fixed.

In beginning it is well to undertake only a small design, so that no great amount of material or time need be consumed in gaining the first experience, but this small piece of work should be carried through to the end, however defective it may become at any stage. A small key-block and two or three colour patches may all be cut on the two sides of one plank for this purpose.

There is great diversity of opinion as to the conventions that are appropriate to the designing of colour prints. In the work of the Japanese masters the convention does not vary. A descriptive black or grey line is used throughout the design, outlining all forms or used as flat spots or patches. The line is not always uniform, but is developed with great subtlety to suggest the character of the form expressed, so that the subsequent flat mass of colour printed within the line appears to be modelled. This treatment of the line is one of the great resources of the work, and is special to this kind of design, in which the line has to be cut with the knife on both sides, and is for this reason capable of unusual development in its power of expressing form. Indeed the knife is the final instrument in the drawing of the design.

Typical examples of key-block impressions are given on pages 26 and 33: they show the variety of character and quality possible in the lines and black masses of key-blocks.

The designing of a print depends most of all upon this development of line and black mass in the key-block. The colour pattern of the print is held together by it, and the form suggested. In the Japanese prints the key-block is invariably printed black or grey. Masses intended to be dense black in the finished print are printed first a flat grey by the key-block, and are then printed a full black from a colour-block like any other patch of colour, the double printing being necessary to give the intensity of the black.

Although several modern prints have been designed on other principles, and sometimes a coloured key-block is successfully used, yet the convention adopted by the Japanese is the simplest and most fundamental of all. Outside its safe limitations the technical difficulties are increased, and one is led to make compromises that strain the proper resources of block printing and are of doubtful advantage.

The temptation to use colour with the key-block comes when one attempts to use the key-block for rendering light and shadow. Its use by the Japanese masters was generally for the descriptive expression of the contours of objects, ignoring entirely their shadows, or any effects of light and shade, unless a shadow happened occasionally to be an important part of the pattern of the design. Generally, as in nearly all the landscape prints by Hiroshig? the line is descriptive or suggestive of essential form, not of effects in light and shade.

If the key-block is used for light and shade, the question of relative tones and values of shadows arises, and these will be falsified unless a key-block is made for each separate plane or part of the design, and then there is danger of confusion or of compromises that are beyond the true scope of the work.

It is generally safest to print the key-block in a tone that blends with the general tone of the print, and not to use it as a part of the colour pattern. It serves mainly to control the form, leaving the colour-blocks to give the colour pattern. There are cases, of course, where no rule holds good, and sometimes a design may successfully omit the key-block altogether, using only a few silhouettes of colour, one of which controls the main form of the print, and serves as key-block. Frequently, also, the key-block may be used to give the interior form or character of part of a design, leaving the shape of a colour-block to express the outside shape or contour; as in the spots suggesting foliage in the print on page 114. The shapes of the tree forms are partly left to the colour-block to complete, the key only giving the suggestion of the general broken character of the foliage, not the outside limits of the branches. The outer shape of a tree or branch is rarely expressed by an enclosing line in any of the Japanese prints. The key-block is often used to describe interior form when a silhouette of colour is all that is needed for the contour. The expressive rendering of the rough surface of tree trunks and of forms of rock, or the articulation of plants and the suggestion of objects in atmospheric distance or mist, should be studied in good prints by the Japanese masters. In printed work by modern masters--as, for example, the work of the great French designers of poster advertisements--much may be learnt in the use and development of expressive line.

The Japanese system of training is well described in a book by Henry P. Bowie on "The Laws of Japanese Painting," in which many useful suggestions are given with reference to graphic brush drawing and the suggestive use of line and brush marks.

As part of the training of a designer for modern decorative printing, the experience and sense of economy that are to be gained from the study of wood-block printing are very great. Perhaps no work goes so directly to the essentials of the art of decorative designing for printed work of all kinds. The wood blocks not only compel economy of design, but also lead one to it.

Even as a means of general training in the elements of decorative pictorial composition the wood blocks have great possibilities as an adjunct to the courses of work followed by art students. The same problems that arise in all decoration may be dealt with by their means on a small scale, but under conditions that are essentially instructive. Colour schemes may be studied and worked out with entire freedom by printing and reprinting until a problem is thoroughly solved. A colour design may be studied and worked out as fully by means of a small set of blocks, and with more freedom for experiment and alteration than is possible by the usual methods of study, such as painting and repainting on paper or canvas or wall; for the form being once established by the blocks, the colour may be reconstructed again and again without limit.

The craft has thus not only its special interest as a means of personal expression, but also a more general use as a means of training and preparation for the wider scope and almost unlimited resources of modern printing. The best use of those resources will be made by artists who have been trained under simpler conditions, and have found their way gradually to an understanding of the secrets of aesthetic economy in printing. One of the many paths to that experience is by way of the craft of the wood-block printer.

CHAPTER VIII

Co-operative Printing

A print is shown at the end of this book (page 95) as an example of a first experiment in co-operative printing. An actual print was needed to illustrate the method of block printing, and the number required was too great for a single printer to undertake. So the work was divided between four printers (of whom the writer was one), working together. Each of us had been accustomed to print our own prints in small batches of a dozen or two at a time, giving individual care to each print. The printing of 2000 prints to a fixed type was a very different matter, and proved an instructive and valuable experience. It was found that the printing of a large number of successive impressions gave one an increasingly delicate control of a block, and a high percentage of perfect impressions. After the initial experiments and practice, the failures in the later batches of the print were reduced to only 4 or 5 per cent. of the completed prints. The work was done in batches of 250 prints, each print receiving eight impressions, as shown on pages 98 to 109. Each of the four printers took charge of a particular series of the blocks, which were printed in a regular order. It was found most convenient to print the key-block last of all, as the heavy blacks in it were inclined to offset under the pressure of the baren and slightly soil the colour-blocks, if the key-block was printed first, as is usually the practice.

The colour-blocks were printed in the order in which they are placed in the Appendix.

The best quality of work was done on nearly dry paper. The damping sheets were placed among the new paper at the end of the day's work and removed after ten or fifteen minutes, the printing paper then was left standing over night between boards, ready for work in the morning, and was not damped again until after receiving several impressions. Then it was very slightly damped again by means of a damping sheet to every ten or twelve prints placed there for a very few minutes.

As one printer finished the impressions from one of his blocks, the batch of papers was passed on to the others, each in turn. In this way three batches of 250 were printed without haste in one week, working eight hours a day for five and a half days.

The chief difficulty experienced was in keeping to the exact colour and quality of the type print, each printer being inclined to vary according to individual preferences. To counteract this tendency, it is necessary for one individual to watch and control the others in these respects.

Otherwise the work proceeded easily and made very clear the possibilities of the craft for the printing of large numbers of prints for special purposes where the qualities required are not obtainable by machine printing. Obviously the best results will always be obtained by the individual printing of his own work by an artist. This can only be done, however, in comparatively small numbers, yet the blocks are capable of printing very large quantities without deterioration. The set of blocks used for the example given here showed very little deterioration after 4000 impressions had been taken. The key-block was less worn than any, the pressure being very slight for this block, and the ink perfectly smooth. The impression of which a reproduction is given on page 109 was taken after 4000 had been printed from the key-block. Block No. 2 was much more worn by the gritty nature of the burnt sienna used in its printing. It would be an easy matter, however, to replace any particular colour-block that might show signs of wear in a long course of printing.

Other examples given in the Appendix show qualities and methods of treatment that are instructive or suggestive.

No. 6 is the key impression of a Japanese print in which an admirable variety of resource is shown by its design; the character of each kind of form being rendered by such simple yet so expressive indications. It is instructive to study the means by which this is done, and to notice how interior form is sometimes suggested by groups of spots or black marks of varied shape while the indication of the external form is left entirely to the shape of the colour-block subsequently to be printed.

Plate XVI is a reproduction of a print by Hiroshig?and shows the suggestive use of the key-block in rendering tree forms. Plates XVII and XVIII show in greater detail this kind of treatment.

Plates XXIII-XXIV are key-blocks of modern print designs.

APPENDIX

An original print in colour, designed and cut by the author and printed by hand on Japanese paper, followed by collotype reproductions showing the separate impressions of the colour blocks used for this print, and other collotype reproductions of various examples of printing and design.

```
+----------------------------------------------------------------------+  |The   particulars
given in Chapter VIII on co-operative printing refer |  |specially to the original
print included in the first edition. In this |  |edition an entirely new print is
shown, and only 1,000 copies of it are|  |being published. | +----------------------
----------------------------------------------+
```

BOOKS OF REFERENCE

"Tools and Materials illustrating the Japanese Method of Colour Printing." A descriptive catalogue of a collection exhibited in the Victoria and Albert Museum, London. Price Twopence. Victoria and Albert Museum Catalogues. 1913.

"The Colour Prints of Japan." By Edward F. Strange. The Langham Series of Art Monographs. London.

"Japanese Colour Prints." By Edward F. Strange. (3rd Edition.) Victoria and Albert Museum Handbooks. London.

"Japanese Wood Engravings." By William Anderson, F. R. C. S. London, Seeley & Co., Ltd. New York, Macmillan & Co. 1895.

"Japanese Wood-cutting and Wood-cut Printing." By T. Tokuno. Edited and annotated by S. R. Kochler. Report of the Smithsonian Institution, Washington, for the year ending June 30, 1892. Issued in pamphlet form by the U.S.A. National Museum, Washington. 1893.

Other works containing descriptions and references to the craft of wood-block printing in the Art Library at the Victoria and Albert Museum, London, are the following:--

"The Industries of Japan." By J. J. Rein. (Paper, pp. 389.) London. 1889.

"Bungei Ruisan," By Yoshino Sakakibara. Essays on Japanese literature, with additional chapters describing the manufacture of paper and the processes of printing and engraving. (The Museum copy has MS. translations of the portion relating to engraving.) Tokyo. 1878.

Made in the USA
Middletown, DE
16 January 2023

22285648R00029